Jelly Roll Jambalaya
Quilts

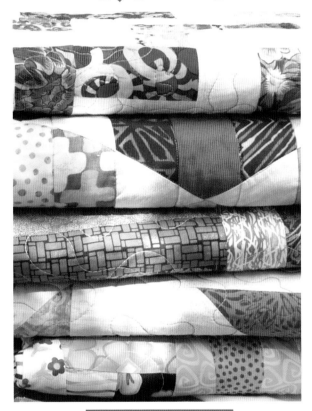

by Jean Ann Wright

Landauer Publishing, an imprint of Fox Chapel Publishing

Jelly Roll Jambalaya
Quilts
by Jean Ann Wright

Landauer Publishing is an imprint of Fox Chapel Publishing Company, Inc.

Editor: Jeri Simon
Art Director: Laurel Albright
Photographer: Sue Voegtlin

We are always looking for talented authors. To submit an idea,
please send a brief inquiry to acquisitions@foxchapelpublishing.com.

Printed in Singapore

10 9 8 7 6 5 4 3 2

ISBN: 978-1-935726-49-4

Introduction

Simple quilts with an eye to color and design that can be sewn quickly for instant gratification are the factors I consider when starting a new quilting project. The jelly roll quilts and quilts made from 2-1/2" pre-cuts in this book fit that criteria. Putting this book together has been loads of fun, almost as much fun as making the quilts.

Before the idea of the book came about, I began purchasing jelly roll and 2-1/2" pre-cut bundles with no particular plan in mind. Thoughts began to form on how I could fully utilize each bundle. A bundle of 40 strips will make a 48" x 60" quilt if every strip is used. I soon realized I didn't need to use every strip in a single quilt. Some strips could be set aside for other projects or binding. Yardage could be added to the quilt to make a unified background or create borders to increase the size of the quilt.

As I started sewing the quilts, I realized different quilting methods or techniques were being used in many of the quilts. in each quilt. These are highlighted in La Petite Lessons.

Quilting should be fun…loads of it! Playing with color and fabric is a great way to let the creative mind flow. The only limitation is your imagination.

Happy stripping!
Jean Ann

◆◆◆◆◆◆◆◆◆◆◆

About the Author

Jean Ann Wright has been sewing and making quilts for over 25 years. She majored in textiles and fine arts at Palm Beach State College and has combined these two disciplines to become a fiber artist. From 1986 to 2006 she edited an international quilting magazine titled QUILT, plus a variety of special-interest quilting titles with the same publishing company.

Jean Ann is the co-author of *Circle of Nine, Log Cabin Quilts The basics & beyond* and *Quilting a Circle of Nine*. She is the author of *Quilt Sashings & Settings The basics & beyond* and is the designer of several specialty rulers from Creative Grids®.

Contents

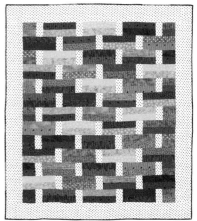
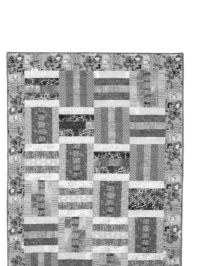

Contents

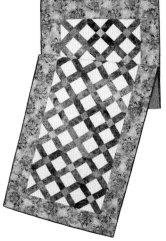
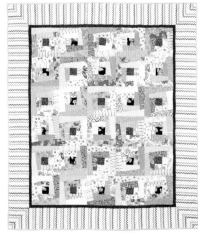
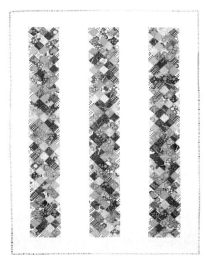

Baby King Cakes Quilt

In New Orleans a king cake is associated with the pre-Lenten celebrations of Mardi Gras. The cake has a tiny trinket, often a small plastic baby, baked inside. The piece of cake with the trinket has various privileges and obligations. Most often, the person who finds the "baby" in their piece of cake is the "king" of next year's celebration. The blocks in this quilt show our jelly roll cake divided into individual bite size pieces, each one a little baby king cake.

Fabric Requirements

- 1 Jelly Roll bundle containing 40 strips
- 1/3 yard inner border fabric
- 2 yards border and binding fabric
- 4-1/4 yards backing fabric
- Twin-size batting

(80) 6" x 6" Patience Corner Blocks
Finished quilt size 60" x 72"

Jelly Roll strip = 2-1/2" x WOF

WOF = Width of fabric

LOF = Length of fabric

NOTE: Sew with a scant 1/4" seam allowance

Cutting and Sewing the Blocks

From each jelly roll strip, cut
  (8)—2-1/2" x 4-1/2" rectangles and
  (2) 2-1/2" squares.

Use 4 matching 2-1/2" x 4-1/2" rectangles and
  1 contrasting 2-1/2" square to make a
  Patience Corner block.
  Make a total of 80 blocks.

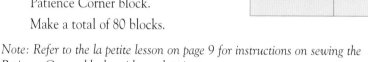

Note: Refer to the la petite lesson on page 9 for instructions on sewing the Patience Corner blocks with overlapping seams.

Quilt Assembly

1. Referring to the Quilt Assembly Diagram on page 8, lay out the blocks in 10 rows with 8 blocks in each row.

2. Sew the blocks together in rows. Sew the rows together to complete the quilt center.

3. From the inner border fabric, cut (6) 1-1/2" x WOF strips. Sew the strips together to make one continuous strip. From the continuous strip, cut (2) 1-1/2" x 60" side inner borders and (2) 1-1/2" x 50-1/2" top/bottom borders. Sew the side inner borders to opposite sides of the quilt center. Trim away any excess fabric. Sew the side top/bottom borders to the top and bottom of the quilt center. Trim away any excess fabric. Press seams toward borders.

4. From the border/binding fabric, cut (4) 5-1/2" x LOF strips for borders. Trim the strips to 60-1/2"-long. Sew 2 border strips to opposite sides of the quilt center and trim even with quilt center. Sew the remaining 2 border strips to the top/bottom of the quilt center and trim.

Baby King Cakes Quilt

Quilt designed and made by Jean Ann Wright
Jelly Roll fabrics: Flirt by Sandy Gervais for Moda Fabrics

5. From the border/binding fabric, cut (6) 2-1/4" x LOF strips. Sew the strips together end-to-end to make one continuous binding strip.

Finishing

Layer the quilt top, batting and backing. Baste the layers together. Hand or machine quilt as desired. Bind the edges to finish.

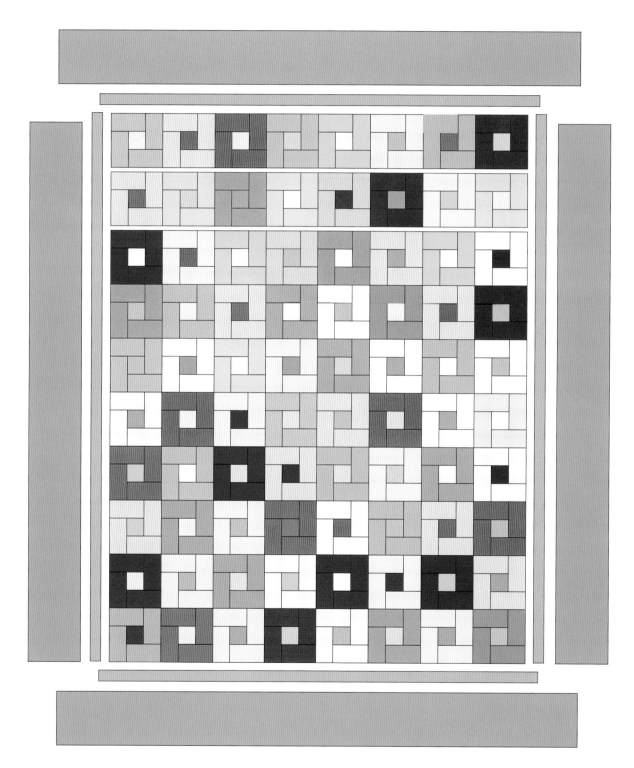

Quilt Assembly Diagram

:La Petite Lesson:

Overlapping Seams

Many sewing tasks call for overlapping seams. While overlapping seams may look complicated to sew, there is an easy way to create the blocks that will make you an expert in no time.

1 Lay a 2-1/2" square on a 2-1/2" x 4-1/2" rectangle, right sides together. Referring to the illustration, stitch a partial seam approximately 1-3/4" long.

2 Fold the square out and press seams toward the square to make unit A.

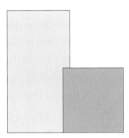

3 Lay a 2-1/2" x 4-1/2" rectangle on the adjacent side of unit A. Stitch the pieces together as shown. Press rectangle open to make unit B.

4 Sew a 2-1/2" x 4-1/2" rectangle to unit B as shown. Press rectangle open to make unit C.

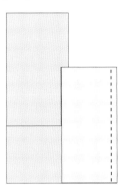

5 Sew a 2-1/2" x 4-1/2" rectangle to the remaining side of unit C taking care to fold the first rectangle away from the square as you stitch. (You do not want to catch it in the seam.) Press rectangle open.

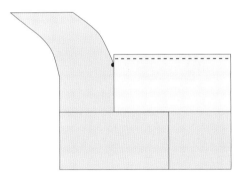

6 Fold the first rectangle over the square and the last rectangle you added. Finish sewing the partial seam to complete the block. Press.

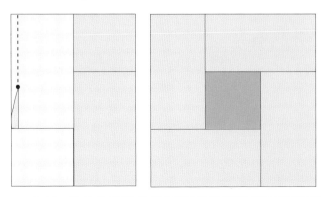

Streetcars Quilt

Translating any design element into a quilt is second nature to most quilters, so making subway tiles into a quilt block was an easy transition. New Orleans is known for its colorful streetcars that run on tracks taking visitors throughout the historic district.

Fabric Requirements

1 pre-cut bundle of 2-1/2" strips
NOTE: *You will use 33 of the (40) 2-1/2" strips.*

1-1/2 yards polka dot fabric

3-3/4 yards backing fabric

Twin-size batting

---

(45) 4" x 10" Blocks
(14) 4" x 4" Row End Blocks
Finished quilt size 56" x 62"

Pre-cut bundle = 2-1/2" x WOF strips

WOF = Width of fabric

NOTE: *Sew with a scant 1/4" seam allowance*

Cutting and Sewing the Blocks

1. Separate 26 of the pre-cut strips into 13 sets of two. The sets should use the same color in different values and prints.

2. Set aside 7 pre-cut strips for the binding.

3. Sew the sets of strips together to make a double strip set that measures 4-1/2" x WOF. Make 13 double strip sets. Press seams.

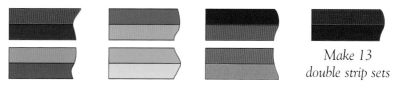

Make 13 double strip sets

4. Subcut the strip sets at 10-1/2" intervals to make (4) 4-1/2" x 10-1/2" blocks from each double strip set. Cut a total of (52) 4-1/2" x 10-1/2" blocks. Set 45 blocks aside.
   TIP: *I used a 10-1/2" square ruler when cutting the blocks. This ensured that each block was cut at the correct interval.*

Make 52

5. Subcut each of the 7 remaining blocks into (2) 4-1/2" x 4-1/2" row end blocks. Cut a total of (14) row end blocks.

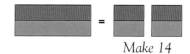

Make 14

6. Using the polka dot fabric, cut (3) 4-1/2" x WOF strips. Subcut the strips into (46) 2-1/2" x 4-1/2" rectangles.

Streetcars Quilt

Quilt designed and made by Jean Ann Wright
Pre-cut fabric bundle: Brights by Blank Quilting
Border fabric: Polka Dots by Blank Quilting

Quilt Assembly

1. Referring to the Quilt Assembly Diagram, lay out the blocks, row end blocks and 2-1/2" x 4-1/2" rectangles as shown.

2. Sew the pieces together in rows. Each odd-numbered row will begin and end with a row end block and contain 3 blocks and (4) 2-1/2" x 4-1/2" rectangles. Make 7 odd-numbered rows. Each even-numbered row will contain 4 blocks and (3) 2-1/2" x 4-1/2" rectangles. Make 6 even-numbered rows.

3. Sew the rows together to make the quilt center.

4. From the polka dot fabric, cut (7) 5-1/2" x WOF strips. Sew the strips together end-to-end to make one continuous strip. Subcut the strip into (2) 5-1/2" x 52-1/2" side border strips and (2) 5-1/2" x 56-1/2" top/bottom border strips.

5. Sew the side border strips to opposite sides of the quilt center. Sew the top/bottom strips to the top and bottom of the quilt center to complete the quilt top.

6. Sew the 7 pre-cut strips together end-to-end to make one continuous binding strip.

Finishing

Layer the quilt top, batting and backing. Baste the layers together. Hand or machine quilt as desired. Bind the edges to finish.

Quilt Assembly Diagram

Speedy Strip Piecing

Strip piecing is a great time-saving technique that all quilters will find useful. Several blocks are created with strips—rail fence, nine-patch, four-patch—and the Streetcars, French Quarter and Bourbon Street Bricks quilts all use this technique. Jelly roll and 2-1/2" pre-cut strips are perfect for strip piecing.

1 Sew strips together along the long edge of the fabric. Press the seams. Strip piecing can be used to join two, five or as many strips as needed to create your block.

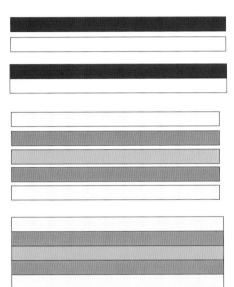

2 Using a quilter's ruler and rotary cutter, subcut the strips the width required in your quilt instructions. The number of segments you will be able to cut from each strip set will be determined by the width of the segment. For example, you will be able to cut (9) 4-1/2"-wide segments from one strip set and (4) 10-1/2"-wide segments from one strip set.

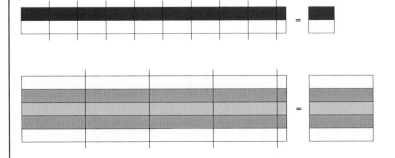

3 The strip set segments can now be used to create blocks or to place in your quilt setting.

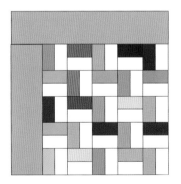

Tip

Having a "tool box" full of rulers in various sizes and shapes helps prevent cutting mistakes. Using a ruler that is just the right size makes quick and accurate cuts every time.

Bourbon Street Bricks Quilt

These richly printed fabrics make a big, bold brick-like pattern. This quilt top was put together in an afternoon. Turn the quilt into a double, queen or king-size bed quilt simply by using additional pre-cut strips. You can also rearrange the strips to make a stunning bed runner.

Fabric Requirements

1 pre-cut bundle of 2-1/2" strips
NOTE: You will use 30 of the (40) 2-1/2" strips.

1-3/4 yards border fabric

1/2 yard contrasting binding fabric

3-1/2 yards backing fabric

Twin-size batting

---

(24) 10" x 10" Blocks:
Finished quilt size 50" x 70"

Pre-cut bundle = 2-1/2" x WOF strips

WOF = Width of fabric

LOF = Length of fabric

NOTE: Sew with a scant 1/4" seam allowance

Cutting and Sewing the Blocks

1. Separate the 30 pre-cut strips into 6 sets with 5 strips in each set. Each strip set should have (2) light value strips, (2) medium/dark value strips and (1) contrasting strip.

2. Sew a set of five strips together with the light value strips on the outside edges, the medium/dark value strips against the light strips and the contrasting strip in the center to make a 10-1/2" x WOF strip set. Press seams. Make 6 strip sets.

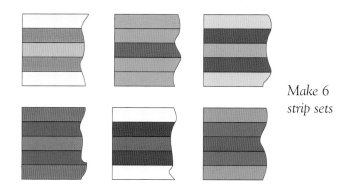

Make 6 strip sets

3. Cut the strip sets at 10-1/2" intervals to make (4) 10-1/2" blocks from each strip set. Cut a total of (24) 10-1/2" blocks.
   TIP: I used a 10-1/2" square ruler when cutting the blocks. This ensured that each block was cut at the correct interval.

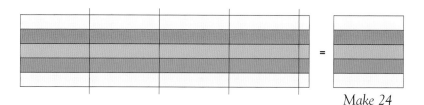

Make 24

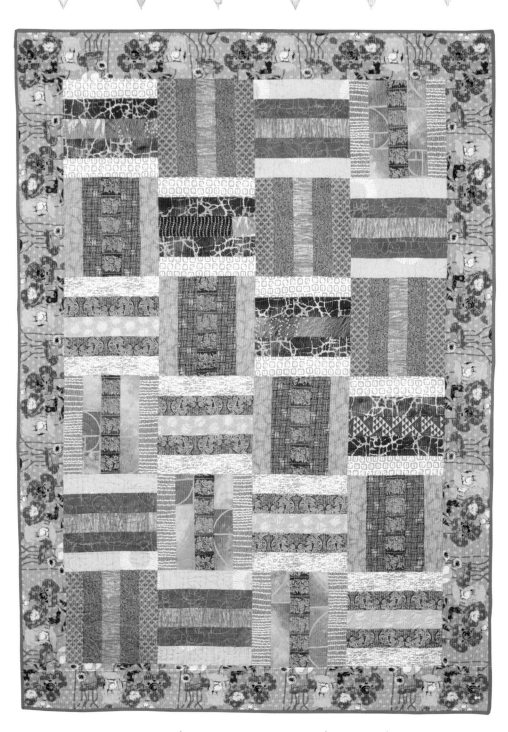

Bourbon Street Bricks Quilt

Quilt designed and made by Jean Ann Wright
Pre-cut fabric bundle: Pink and Teal by Lonni Rossi for Andover Fabrics
Border fabric: Field Study #1 by Anna Maria Horner for Free Spirit

Quilt Assembly

1. Referring to the Quilt Assembly Diagram, lay out the blocks in 6 rows with 4 blocks in each row. Position the blocks in a planned or random manner, whichever you prefer. Sew the blocks together in rows.

2. Sew the rows together to make the quilt center.

3. From the border fabric, cut (4) 5-1/2" x LOF strips. Cut (2) 60-1/2"-long strips for the side borders and (2) 50-1/2"-long strips for the top/bottom borders.

4. Sew the side border strips to opposite sides of the quilt center. Sew the top/bottom strips to the top and bottom of the quilt center to complete the quilt top.

5. From the contrasting binding fabric, cut (7) 2-1/4" x LOF strips. Sew the strips together end-to-end to make one continuous binding strip.

Finishing

Layer the quilt top, batting and backing. Baste the layers together. Hand or machine quilt as desired. Bind the edges to finish.

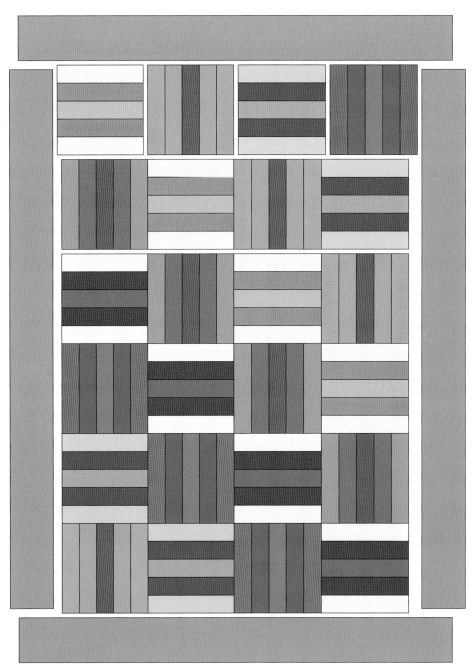

Quilt Assembly Diagram

:La Petite Lesson:

Re-sizing the Quilt

The simplest way to increase the size of a quilt is to add borders or additional rows of blocks. In this case, I used extra pre-cut bundles to stitch up the fast strip-pieced blocks and build more rows. If you want to decrease the size of the quilt, take rows away.

Double or Queen-Size Bed Runner

Finished bed runner size: 40" x 80"

1 pre-cut bundle of 2-1/2" strips

1-1/2 yards border fabric

1/2 yard binding fabric

Cut borders 5-1/2"-wide

Make 24 blocks.

Sew blocks in 3 rows of 8 blocks each.

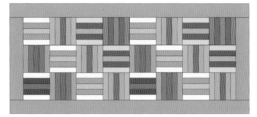

Double or Queen-Size Bed Runner

Double-size Bed Quilt

Finished quilt size: 72" x 92"

2 pre-cut bundles of 2-1/2" strips

2 yards border fabric

2/3 yard binding fabric

Cut borders 6-1/2"-wide

Make 48 blocks.

Sew blocks in 8 rows of 6 blocks each.

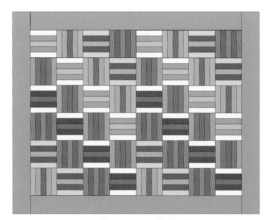

Double-size Bed Quilt

Queen or King-size Bed Quilt

Finished quilt size: 94" x 104"

3 pre-cut bundles of 2-1/2" strips

2-1/2 yards border fabric

2/3 yard binding fabric

Cut (8) 7-1/2"-wide border strips

Make 72 blocks.

Sew blocks in 8 rows of 9 blocks each.

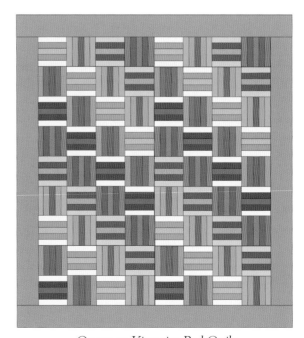

Queen or King-size Bed Quilt

The French Quarter Quilt

Kaffe Fassett's fabrics, with their opulent design and rich colors, are a wonderful addition to any quilt, so I was particularly delighted to find a pre-cut bundle of his print fabrics. The name of the block in the quilt is London Stairs. I took the liberty of naming the quilt The French Quarter because the "stairs" remind me of the popular outside stairways leading to second floor balconies in New Orleans' French Quarter.

Fabric Requirements

1 pre-cut bundle of 2-1/2" strips
NOTE: You will use 20 of the (30) 2-1/2" strips.

1-1/2 yards white fabric

1-3/4 yards border and binding fabric

3-2/3 yards backing fabric

Twin-size batting

---

(180) 4" x 4" Stair Blocks
Finished quilt size 58" x 70"

Pre-cut bundle = 2-1/2" x WOF strips

WOF = Width of fabric

LOF = Length of fabric

NOTE: Sew with a scant 1/4" seam allowance

Cutting and Sewing the Blocks

1. From the white fabric, cut (20) 2-1/2" strips.

2. Layer a white strip and a pre-cut 2-1/2" strip, right sides together, and sew along one long edge to make a strip set measuring 4-1/2" x WOF. Press the seams. Make 20 strip sets.

3. Cut the strip sets at 4-1/2" intervals to make (9) 4-1/2" blocks from each strip set. Cut a total of (180) 4-1/2" blocks.

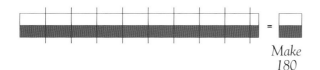

Make 180

4. Place the matching 4-1/2" blocks into piles. You should have 20 piles of identical 4-1/2" blocks.

Quilt Assembly

1. Referring to the photograph on page 19, use a flat surface or design wall and arrange the blocks in 15 rows of 12 blocks each. Carefully watch the orientation of the blocks to create the "stairs".
   NOTE: The (8) even-numbered rows begin with a vertical block orientation. The (7) odd-numbered rows begin with a horizontal block orientation.

2. Sew the blocks together in rows. Sew the rows together to make the quilt center.

3. From the border fabric, cut (7) 5-1/2" x LOF strips. Sew the strips together end-to-end to make one continuous strip. Subcut the strip into (2) 5-1/2" x 60-1/2" side borders and (2) 5-1/2" x 58-1/2" top/bottom borders.

4. Sew the side border strips to opposite sides of the quilt center. Sew the top/bottom strips to the top and bottom of the quilt center to complete the quilt top.

5. From the binding fabric, cut (7) 2-1/4" x LOF strips. Sew the strips together end-to-end to make one continuous binding strip

Finishing

Layer the quilt top, batting and backing. Baste the layers together. Hand or machine quilt as desired. Bind the edges to finish.

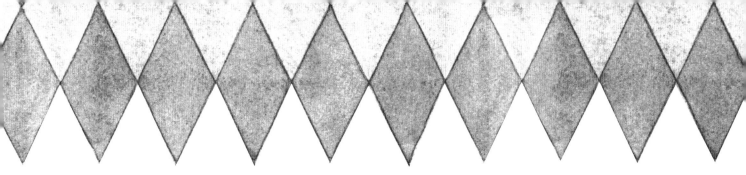

The French Quarter Quilt

Quilt designed and made by Jean Ann Wright
Pre-cut fabric bundle: Kaffe Fassett Classics Blue by Kaffe Fassett for Westminster Fabrics
Border fabric: Dimples by Gail Kessler for Andover

Andouille Quilt

These pre-cut strips are the color of the many different spices that make jambalaya a savory favorite during Mardi Gras.

Fabric Requirements

- 1 pre-cut bundle of (40) 2-1/2" strips
- 1/2 yard red batik binding fabric
- 3-1/2 yards backing fabric
- Twin-size batting

Finished quilt size 48" x 60"

Pre-cut bundle = 2-1/2" x WOF strips

WOF = Width of fabric

LOF = Length of fabric

NOTE: Sew with a scant 1/4" seam allowance

Cutting and Sewing the Blocks

1. Sew the 40 pre-cut strips together end-to-end using 45-degree diagonal seams. You will have one long, continuous strip approximately 1600" in length.

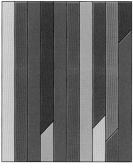

2. From the continuous strip, cut:
   (10) 65-1/2"-long strips
   (4) 40-1/2"-long strips
   (20) 20-1/2"-long strips
   (12) 28-1/2" long strips

3. Sew the (10) 65-1/2"-long strips together along the long edges to make a large rectangle. Trim the large rectangle to 20-1/2" x 65". Cut the rectangle into a 20-1/2" x 24-1/2" rectangle and a 20-1/2" x 40-1/2" rectangle.

20-1/2" x 24-1/2"

20-1/2" x 40-1/2"

Andouille Quilt

Quilt designed and made by Jean Ann Wright
Pre-cut fabric bundle: Berry Mango from Batiks Etcetera

4. Sew the (4) 40-1/2"-long strips together along the long edges. Sew the joined strips to one side of the 20-1/2" x 40-1/2" rectangle from step 3 to make a 28-1/2" x 40-1/2" rectangle.

28-1/2" x 40-1/2"

5. Sew the (20) 20-1/2"-long strips together along the long edges to make a 20-1/2" x 40-1/2" rectangle.

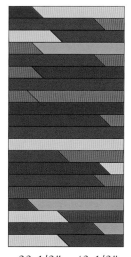

20-1/2" x 40-1/2"

6. Sew the (12) 28-1/2"-long strips together along the long edges to make a 24-1/2" x 28-1/2" rectangle.

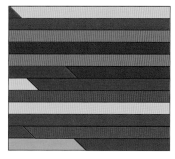

24-1/2" x 28-1/2"

Quilt Assembly

1. Referring to the Quilt Assembly Diagram, lay out the 4 rectangles as shown.

2. Sew the rectangles together in pairs. Sew the pairs together to complete the quilt top.

Finishing

1. Layer the quilt top, batting and backing. Baste the layers together. Hand or machine quilt as desired.

2. From the binding fabric, cut (6) 2-1/4" x width of fabric strips. Sew the strips together end-to-end to make one continuous binding strip. Fold the strip in half lengthwise with wrong sides together and press. Bind the quilt edges to finish.

Quilt Assembly Diagram

:La Petite Lesson:

Diagonal Seams

Diagonal seams are used to join narrow strips of fabric together. These strips are used to make blocks, borders, and bindings. Using diagonal seams reduces bulk and creates a less noticeable transition from one strip to another.

1 Place one fabric strip, right side up, on a flat surface. Place another strip, wrong side up, at a right angle on the first strip as shown.

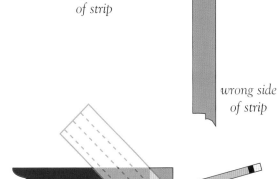

right side
of strip

wrong side
of strip

2 Using a marking pencil and ruler, draw a diagonal line on the top strip as shown.

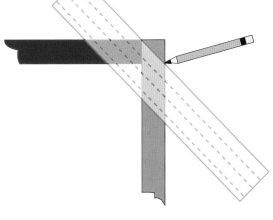

3 Stitch on the drawn line. Using a sharp scissors or rotary cutter, trim 1/4" from the stitched line.

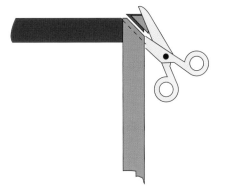

4 Press the seams open. Snip the small fabric 'tails' even with the edge of the strips.

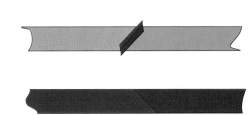

Rémoulade Stars Quilt

Rémoulade is a condiment flavored with a variety of spices. The spicy colors of the blocks create a tessellating design. When stitched together, the bright and light stars interweave to create a positive and negative pattern.

Fabric Requirements

Quilt

Note: To make this quilt the 2-1/2" strips must be 44" long.

1 pre-cut bundle of bright 2-1/2" strips
Note: You will use 20 of the (40) 2-1/2" x 44" strips

1 pre-cut bundle of light 2-1/2" strips
Note: You will use 20 of the (40) 2-1/2" x 44" strips

2 yards beige/cream batik fabric for border and binding fabric

4 yards backing fabric

Double-size batting

---

(20) 12" x 12" Blocks
Finished quilt size 64" x 76"

Pre-cut bundle = 2-1/2" x 44" strips

WOF = width of fabric

LOF = length of fabric

NOTE: *Sew with a scant 1/4" seam allowance*

Bed Runner
Double or Queen-Size

Finished Size: 44" x 80"

1 pre-cut bundle of bright 2-1/2" strips
Note: You will use 20 of the (40) 2-1/2" x 44" strips

1 pre-cut bundle of light 2-1/2" strips
Note: You will use 20 of the (40) 2-1/2" x 44" strips

1-1/2 yards beige/cream batik fabric for border

1/2 yard binding fabric

Cut borders 4-1/2" wide

Make 18 blocks. Sew blocks in 3 rows of 6 blocks each.

Cutting and Sewing the Blocks

Note: Each star block is cut from 1 light strip and 1 bright strip.

1. Carefully cut each of the (20) light strips and (20) bright strips into (4) 6-1/2" segments and (4) 4-1/2" segments.

6-1/2"	6-1/2"	6-1/2"	6-1/2"	4-1/2"	4-1/2"	4-1/2"	4-1/2"

Rémoulade Stars Quilt

Quilt designed and made by Jean Ann Wright
Pre-cut fabric bundle: Batik Story Strips from Anthology Fabrics and
Lucky Potato by Island Batik

2. Place a light 4-1/2" fabric strip, right side up, on a flat surface. Place a bright strip, wrong side up, at a right angle on the light strip as shown. Using a marking pencil and ruler, draw a diagonal line on the top strip.

3. Stitch on the drawn line. Trim 1/4" from the stitched line. Press the seams open to make a pieced unit. Make 80 pieced units.

Make 80

4. Sew a light 6-1/2" strip and a bright 6-1/2" strip to opposite long edges of a pieced unit to make a quarter unit. Refer to the diagram to ensure the correct position of the strips. Make 80 quarter units.

Make 80

5. Referring to the diagram, sew four quarter units together to complete a block. Make 20 blocks.

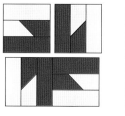 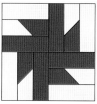

Make 20

Quilt Assembly

1. Referring to the Quilt Assembly Diagram on page 27, lay out the blocks in 5 rows with 4 blocks in each row. Sew the blocks together in rows.

2. Sew the rows together to complete the quilt center.

3. From the beige/cream batik border fabric, cut (4) 8-1/2" x LOF strips. Cut (2) 60-1/2"-long strips for the side borders and (2) 76-1/2"-long strips for the top/bottom borders.

4. Sew the side borders to opposite sides of the quilt center. Sew the top/bottom borders to the top and bottom of the quilt center to complete the quilt top.

Finishing

1. Layer the quilt top, batting and backing. Baste the layers together. Hand or machine quilt as desired.

2. From the remaining beige/cream batik fabric, cut (8) 2-1/4" x LOF binding strips. Sew the strips together end-to-end to make one continuous binding strip. Fold the strip in half lengthwise with wrong sides together and press. Bind the quilt edges to finish.

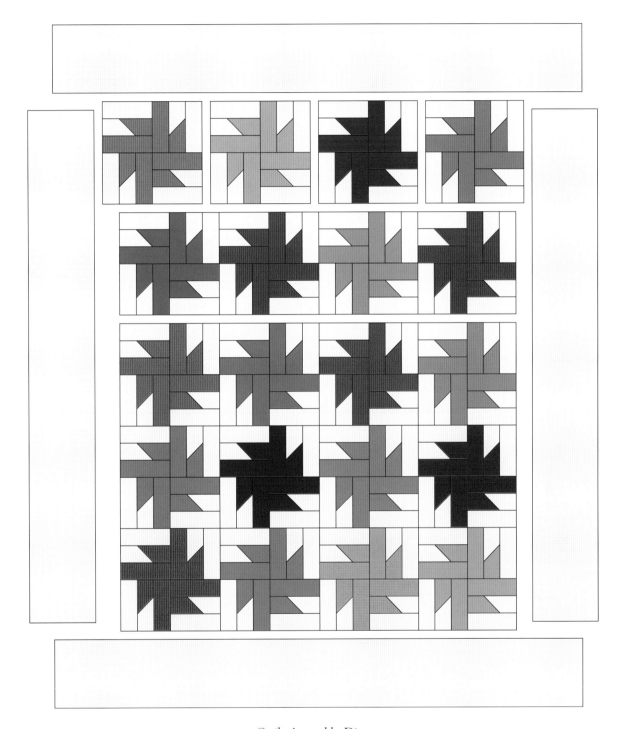

Quilt Assembly Diagram

Mardi Gras Throws Quilt

Modern prints in bright colors make a bold statement—perfect for sewing rows of hexagon Mardi Gras throws. What are throws? Beads of course, strings and strings of beads. During Mardi Gras these inexpensive trinkets are tossed from parade floats in response to cries from the spectators yelling, "Throw me something, throw me something!"

Fabric Requirements

1 Jelly Roll bundle
Note: You will use 39 of the (40) 2-1/2" strips

2 yards triangle and border fabric

2/3 yard contrasting binding fabric

4 yards backing fabric

Twin-size batting

---

(65) 6-7/8" x 6" Blocks
Finished quilt size 56" x 66"

Jelly Roll strip = 2-1/2" x WOF

WOF = Width of fabric

LOF = Length of fabric

NOTE: Sew with a scant 1/4" seam allowance

Cutting and Sewing the Blocks

1. Sew 3 Jelly Roll strips together along the long edges as shown. Press the seams open to make a strip set. Make 13 strip sets.

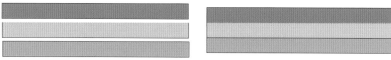

Make 13

2. Use the hexagon template on page 33 or refer to the la petite lesson on pages 34-35 to cut 5 hexagons from each strip set. Cut a total of 65 hexagons from the strip sets.

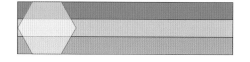

Cut 65

3. Using the remaining pieces of strip sets from step 2, cut 10 partial hexagons using the template on page 32.

Cut 10

4. From the triangle fabric, cut (11) 3-3/4" x width of fabric strips. Use the triangle template on page 32 or refer to the la petite lesson, Cutting 60-degree Triangles on page 35 to cut triangles from each strip. Cut a total of 150 triangles.

Cut 150

Mardi Gras Throws Quilt

Quilt designed and made by Jean Ann Wright
Jelly Roll fabrics: Simple Marks Summer by Maria Dubrawsky for Moda Fabrics
Border fabric: Basic Gray by Moda Fabrics

5. Sew a triangle to opposite sides of a hexagon as shown to make a hexagon block. Make 65 hexagon blocks.

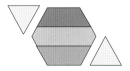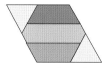

Make 65

6. Sew a triangle to one side of a partial hexagon as shown to make a partial hexagon block. Make 10 partial hexagon blocks.

Make 10

Quilt Assembly

1. Referring to the Quilt Assembly diagram onpage 31, lay out the partial hexagon blocks, the hexagon blocks and the triangles in 10 rows as shown.

Note: The odd numbered rows begin and end with a partial hexagon block and the even numbered rows begin and end with a hexagon block and triangles.

2. Sew the pieces together in rows. Sew the rows together matching the seams of the triangles and hexagons.

3. Using a rotary cutter and ruler, cut the ends of the rows so the partial hexagon blocks and triangles are trimmed in an even line to complete the quilt center.

Trim line   *Trim line*

4. From the border fabric, cut (6) 4-1/2" x WOF strips. Sew the strips together end-to-end to form a continuous strip. From the strip, cut (2) 4-1/2" x 55-1/2"strips for the top and bottom borders and (2) 4-1/2" x 59" strips for the side borders. Sew the side borders to opposite sides of the quilt center. Sew the top and bottom borders to the top and bottom of the quilt center to complete the quilt top.

Finishing

1. Layer the quilt top, batting and backing. Baste the layers together. Hand or machine quilt as desired.

2. From the contrasting binding fabric, cut (7) 2-1/4" x LOF binding strips. Sew the strips together end-to-end to make one continuous binding strip. Fold the strip in half lengthwise with wrong sides together and press. Bind the quilt edges to finish.

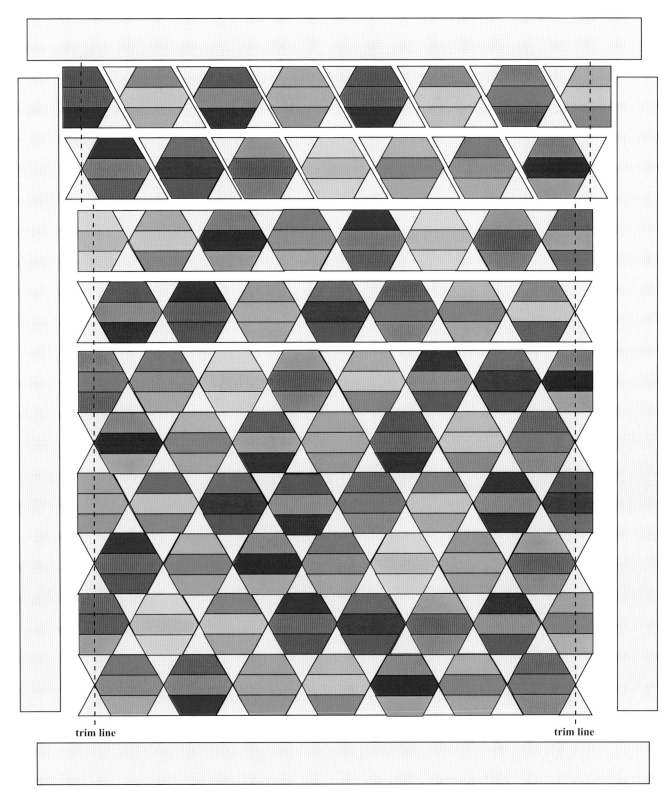

trim line   trim line

Quilt Assembly Diagram

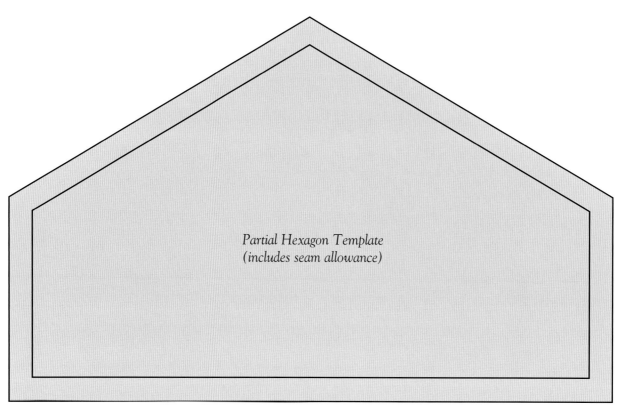

Partial Hexagon Template
(includes seam allowance)

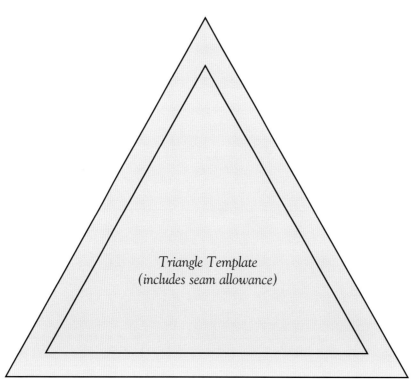

Triangle Template
(includes seam allowance)

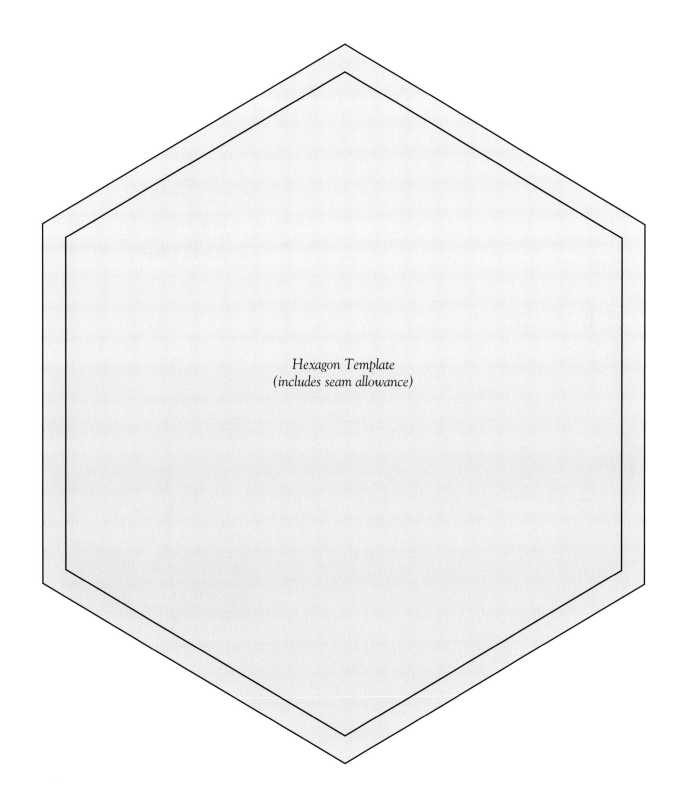

Hexagon Template
(includes seam allowance)

:La Petite Lesson:

Cutting Hexagons and 60-degree Triangles

Modern quilters are rediscovering the hexagon shape and its many possibilities for creative design. While many templates are available for cutting perfect hexagons, they can also be cut using a standard quilter's ruler. These rulers are marked with 45- and 60-degree angles for cutting triangles and other angled shapes. The hexagon is made using the 60-degree mark.

Cutting Hexagons

1 Sew 3 jelly roll strips together along the long edges to create a strip set. Press the seams open to reduce bulk when cutting. Cut the strip set into (5) 7-1/2" segments. The hexagons will be cut from these segments. Finger-press each segment in half lengthwise.

Tip: Use spray starch to add body to the strip set.

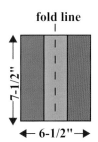

fold line

7-1/2"

← 6-1/2" →

2 Position the 60-degree line on the ruler even with the long edge of the segment. Trim along this angle.

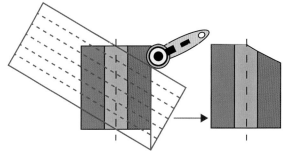

3 To trim the adjacent side of the hexagon, position the 60-degree line of the ruler on the angle cut in step 2. Trim along this angle.

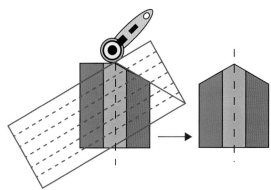

4 Turn the trimmed segment and position the 60-degree line of the ruler on the angle cut in Step 3. Trim along this angle.

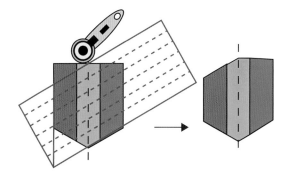

5 Reposition the ruler on the angle cut in step 2. Trim along the angle to complete the hexagon.

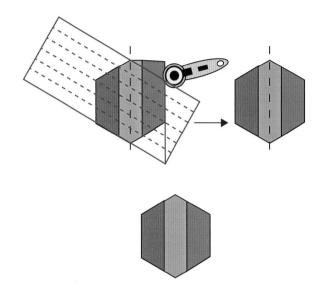

Cutting 60-degree Triangles

1 Cut a 3-3/4" x WOF strip. Position the 60-degree line of the ruler on the top edge of the fabric strip as shown. Trim along the left angle of the ruler.

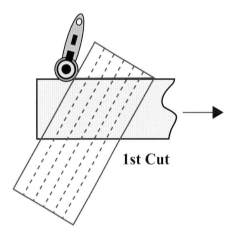

1st Cut

2 Reposition the 60-degree line of the ruler on the angle cut in step 1 as shown. The tip of the ruler should be even with the top of the fabric strip. Cut along the right angle of the ruler to make a triangle.

Note: To make multiple triangles turn the ruler aligning the 60-degree ruler line with the previous cut angle.

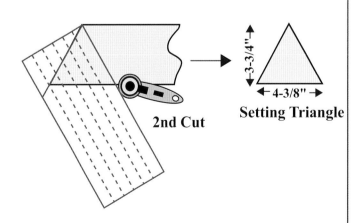

2nd Cut

3-3/4"

4-3/8"

Setting Triangle

Beignet Bed Runner

A beignet is a pastry made from a deep fried batter topped with powdered sugar and served hot. When a fruit-filled beignet is delivered as a breakfast in bed treat, it's simply a taste of heaven. The beignet bed runner is made with colorful batiks that include blueberry, raspberry and banana.

Fabric Requirements

Queen-Size

(33) 8" x 8" Blocks
Finished bed runner size 36" x 100"

1 pre-cut bundle of light 2-1/2" strips
Note: You will use 35 of the (40) 2-1/2" strips

1-1/2 yards cream background fabric

1-1/2 yards tan batik border fabric

2/3 yards contrasting binding fabric

3-1/2 yards backing fabric

Queen-size batting

Pre-cut bundle = 2-1/2" x WOF strips

WOF = Width of fabric

LOF = Length of fabric

NOTE: Sew with a scant 1/4" seam allowance

Bed Runner
Twin or Full-Size

Finished Size: 34" x 82"

1 pre-cut bundle of light 2-1/2" strips
Note: You will use 29 of the (40) 2-1/2" strips

1-1/4 yards of cream background fabric

1 yard border fabric

1/2 yard binding fabric

2-1/2 yards backing fabric

Cut borders 5-1/2" wide

Make 27 blocks. Sew blocks in 3 rows of 9 blocks each.

Cutting and Sewing the Blocks

1. Select 2 light color strips from the pre-cut bundle. Cut a total of (33) 2-1/2" center squares from the strips.

Cut 33

2. From each of the remaining 33 pre-cut strips, cut (4) 2-1/2" x 9" rectangles for a total of 132 rectangles.

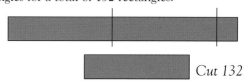
Cut 132

3. From the background fabric, cut (7) 7-1/2" x WOF strips. Subcut each strip into (5) 7-1/2" squares. You will use 33 of the squares.

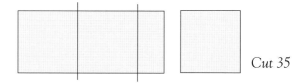
Cut 35

4. Cut a 7-1/2" square in half twice on the diagonal to make 4 quarter-square triangles. Repeat with the (32) 7-1/2" squares for a total of 132 quarter-square triangles.

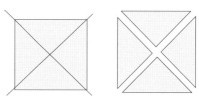
Cut 132

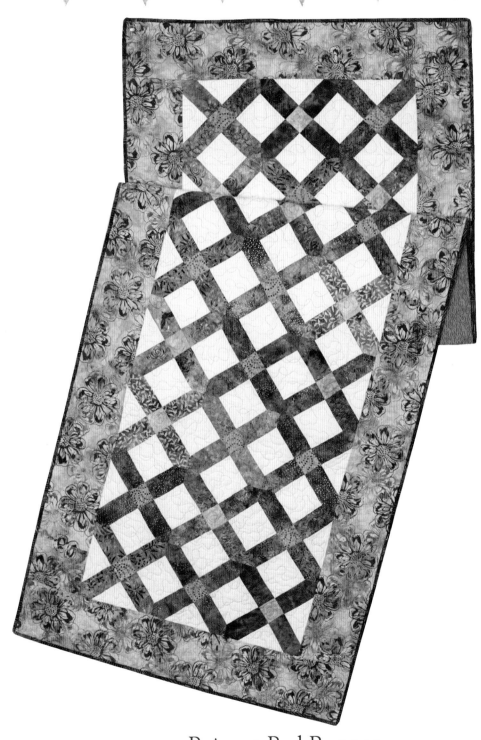

Beignet Bed Runner

Quilt designed and made by Jean Ann Wright
Pre-cut fabric bundle: "Dove Rolls" by Sew Batik
Border fabric: Multi-colored tan batik print

5. To make the block, select a 2-1/2" center square, 4 matching 2-1/2" x 9" rectangles and 4 quarter-square triangles. Sew a 2-1/2" x 9" rectangle to opposite sides of the 2-1/2" center square. Press seams toward square.

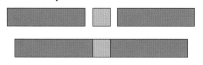

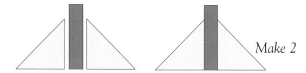

6. Sew a quarter-square triangle to opposite sides of a 2-1/2" x 9" rectangle, aligning the bottom of the triangles with one end of the rectangle. Press seams toward triangles to make an A unit. Make 2 A units.

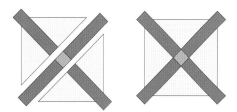

Make 2

7. Lay out the strip made in step 5 and 2 A units as shown. Sew the A units to opposite sides of the strip to make the block. Press seams toward strip.

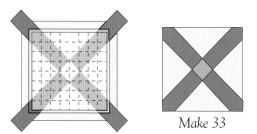

8. Center an 8-1/2" square ruler on the block and trim each side to complete the "X" block. Make 33 "X" blocks.

Make 33

Bed Runner Assembly

1. Referring to the Bed Runner Assembly Diagram, lay out the "X" blocks in 3 rows with 11 blocks in each row. Sew the blocks together in rows.

2. Sew the rows together to complete the bed runner center.

3. From the border fabric, cut (8) 6-1/2" x WOF strips. Sew the strips together end-to-end to form a continuous strip. From the strip, cut

(2) 6-1/2" x 88-1/2" side borders and
(2) 6-1/2" x 45-1/2" end borders.

4. Sew the side borders to the long edges of the bed runner center. Sew the end borders to opposite ends of the bed runner center to complete the bed runner.

Finishing

1. Layer the quilt top, batting and backing. Baste the layers together. Hand or machine quilt as desired.

2. From the contrasting binding fabric, cut (7) 2-1/4" x LOF strips. Sew the strips together end-to-end to make one continuous binding strip. Fold the strip in half lengthwise with wrong sides together and press. Bind the quilt edges to finish.

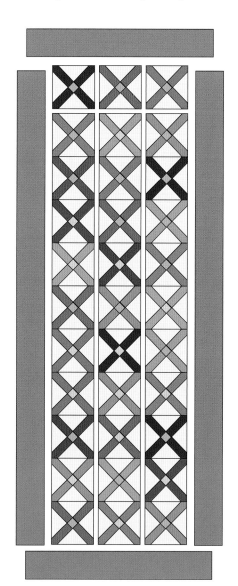

Bed Runner Assembly Diagram

"X" Blocks or Album Blocks

The "X" block, or Album block, is often ignored by quilters because it was originally sewn using templates and cutting each piece individually. Today's quilters want to rotary cut their block pieces for greater accuracy and to save time. The technique shown offers the perfect solution using 2-1/2" strips and one additional fabric.

Note: Pre-cut 2-1/2" strips make this block come together quickly.

1 Cut (1) 2-1/2" center square.

2 Cut (4) matching 2-1/2" x 9" rectangles.

3 Cut (1) 7-1/2" square using a light background fabric. Cut the square in half twice on the diagonal to make 4 quarter-square triangles.

4 Sew a 2-1/2" x 9" rectangle to opposite sides of the 2-1/2" center square.

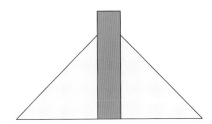

5 Sew a quarter-square triangle to opposite sides of a 2-1/2" x 9" rectangle, aligning the bottom of the triangles with one end of the rectangle. Press seams to make an A unit. Make 2 A units.

6 Sew the A units to opposite sides of the strip made in step 4 to make the block. Press.

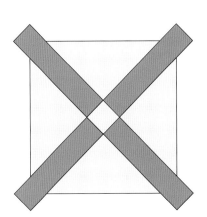

7 Center an 8-1/2" square ruler on the block and trim each side to complete the "X" block.

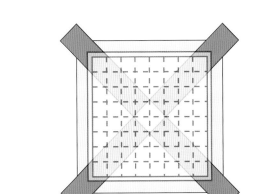

Lagniappe Log Cabin Quilt

Lagniappe is a fascinating word used to describe a small, unexpected gift that says "thank you" in a very special way. If you have shopped in the French Quarter of New Orleans you may have been gifted with a lagniappe from a grateful shop owner or salesperson.

Fabric Requirements

Note: To make this quilt the 2-1/2" strips must be 44"–long without the selvege.

1 Jelly Roll bundle
Note: You will use 37 of the (40) 2-1/2" strips

1-3/4 yards print border fabric

3/4 yard black inner border and binding fabric

3-3/4 yards backing fabric

Twin-size batting

Tools

5-1/2" square ruler

8-1/2" square ruler or Log Cabin Trim Tool

---

(30) 8" x 8" Blocks
Finished quilt size: 54" x 60"

Jelly Roll strip = 2-1/2" x WOF

WOF = Width of fabric

LOF = Length of fabric

NOTE: Sew with a scant 1/4" seam allowance

Cutting and Sewing the Blocks

Note: Press seams toward the outside edges of the block as you sew the strips in place.

1. Select 2 black or dark print strips from the jelly roll bundle. Cut a total of (30) 2-1/2" center squares from the strips.

2. From 15 light print jelly roll strips, cut (2) 2-1/2" squares, (2) 2-1/2" x 4-1/2" rectangles, (2) 2-1/2" x 5-1/2" rectangles and (2) 2-1/2" x 7-1/2" rectangles.

3. From 20 bright print jelly roll strips, cut (1) 2-1/2" x 4-1/2" rectangle, (1) 2-1/2" x 6-1/2" rectangle, (1) 2-1/2" x 7-1/2" rectangle and (1) 2-1/2" x 9-1/2" rectangle.

4. Divide the leftover sections of the bright jelly roll strips into 2 sets of 10 strips. From one set of strips, cut (1) 2-1/2" x 4-1/2" and (1) 2-1/2" x 9-1/2" rectangle. From the remaining set of strips, cut (1) 2-1/2" x 6-1/2" and (1) 2-1/2" x 7-1/2" rectangle.

5. To make the block, sew a 2-1/2" light square to one side of a 2-1/2" black center square. Press to make an A unit.

A unit

6. Sew a 2-1/2" x 4-1/2" light rectangle to one side of the A unit. Press to make a B unit.

B unit

7. Sew a 2-1/2" x 4-1/2" bright rectangle to the B unit as shown. Press to make a C unit.

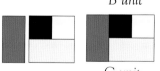

C unit

8. Sew a 2-1/2" x 6-1/2" bright rectangle to the C unit. Press. The black center square should now be surrounded.

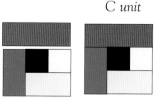

Lagniappe Log Cabin Quilt

Quilt designed and made by Jean Ann Wright
Jelly Roll fabrics: Twirl by Me and My Sister Designs for Moda Fabrics
Border fabric: Ziggy Candy by Timeless Treasures

9. With the right side of the fabric facing up, position the 5-1/2" square ruler on the block, tilting the ruler to the left so each corner of the ruler touches the outside edges of the block. With a rotary cutter, trim around the ruler to make a 5-1/2" center block unit.

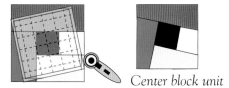

Center block unit

10. Referring to the diagram, sew a 2-1/2" x 5-1/2" light rectangle to the center block unit. Press to make a D unit.

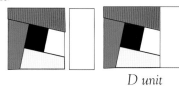

D unit

11. Sew a 2-1/2" x 7-1/2" light rectangle to the adjacent side of the D unit. Press to make an E unit.

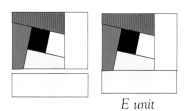

E unit

12. Sew a 2-1/2" x 7-1/2" bright rectangle to the E unit as shown. Press to make an F unit.

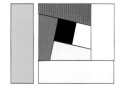 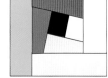

F unit

13. Sew a 2-1/2" x 9-1/2" bright rectangle to the remaining side of the F unit. Press. The 5-1/2" center block should now be surrounded.

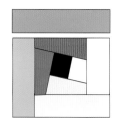 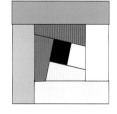

14. With the right side of the fabric facing up, position the 8-1/2" square ruler on the block, tilting the ruler to the right so each corner of the ruler touches the outside edges of the block. With a rotary cutter, trim around the ruler to complete the block. Make 30 blocks.

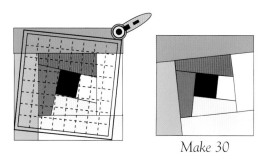

Make 30

Quilt Assembly

Note: Carefully watch the placement of the blocks to create the Straight Furrow Log Cabin setting shown.

1. Referring to the Quilt Center Assembly Diagram lay out the blocks in 6 rows with 5 blocks in each row. Sew the blocks together in rows.

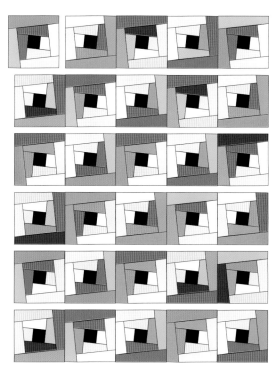

Quilt Center Assembly Diagram

2. Sew the rows together to complete the quilt center.

3. From the black border fabric, cut (3) 1-1/2" x LOF strips. Sew the strips together end-to-end to form a continuous strip. From the strip, cut (2) 1-1/2" x 48-1/2" strips for the side inner borders and (2) 1-1/2" x 42-1/2" strips for the top/bottom inner borders.

4. Referring to the Quilt Assembly Diagram, sew the side inner borders to opposite sides of the quilt center. Sew the top/bottom inner borders to the top and bottom of the quilt center.

5. From the print border fabric, cut (4) 6-1/2" x LOF strips. Fold each border strip in half widthwise end-to-end and press the center fold line. Pin the center of the border strips to the center of the quilt top. Continue to pin toward the outside edges stopping 1/4" from the outside edges of the quilt center. Sew the borders in place, stopping 1/4" from each end. Miter the corners at a 45-degree angle, stitch and trim away the excess fabric.

Finishing

1. Layer the quilt top, batting and backing. Baste the layers together. Hand or machine quilt as desired.

2. From the remaining black fabric, cut (7) 2-1/4" x LOF strips. Sew the strips together end-to-end to make one continuous binding strip. Fold the strip in half lengthwise with wrong sides together and press. Bind the quilt edges to finish.

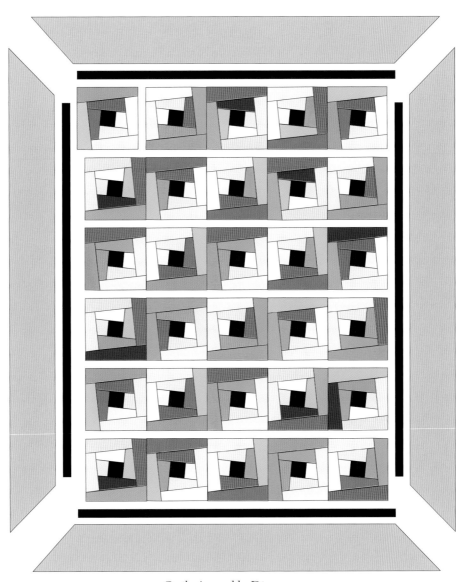

Quilt Assembly Diagram

Carnival Confetti Quilt

What would a carnival like Mardi Gras be without confetti? I made my Carnival Confetti quilt using squares, but many different widths of fabric strips can be used to produce intricate patterns.

Fabric Requirements

1 Jelly Roll bundle containing 40 strips

2-1/4 yards white fabric

4-1/4 yards backing fabric

Twin-size batting

Approximate finished quilt size 55" x 70"

Jelly Roll strip = 2-1/2" x WOF

WOF = Width of fabric

LOF = Length of fabric

NOTE: Sew with a scant 1/4" seam allowance

Cutting and Sewing the Blocks

Note: Separate the jelly roll bundle into 30 bright strips and 10 light or white strips.

1. From 20 bright jelly roll strips, cut each strip into (4) 2-1/2" x 10" rectangles for a total of 80 rectangles.

2. From 7 light or white jelly roll strips, cut each strip into (4) 2-1/2" x 10" rectangles for a total of 28 rectangles.

3. From 1 light or white jelly roll strip, cut (2) 2-1/2" x 10" rectangles and (2) 2-1/2" x 7-1/2" rectangles. Cut the remaining portion of the strip into 2-1/2" squares.

4. Choose (5) 2-1/2" x 10" bright rectangles and (2) 2-1/2" x 10" light rectangles. Sew the rectangles together with a light rectangle on each outside edge as shown. Press to make a strip set. Make 15 strip sets.

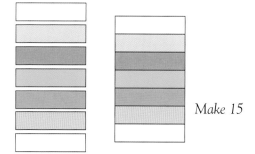

Make 15

5. Cut each strip set into (4) 2-1/2" segments for a total of 60 segments.

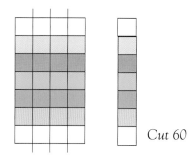

Cut 60

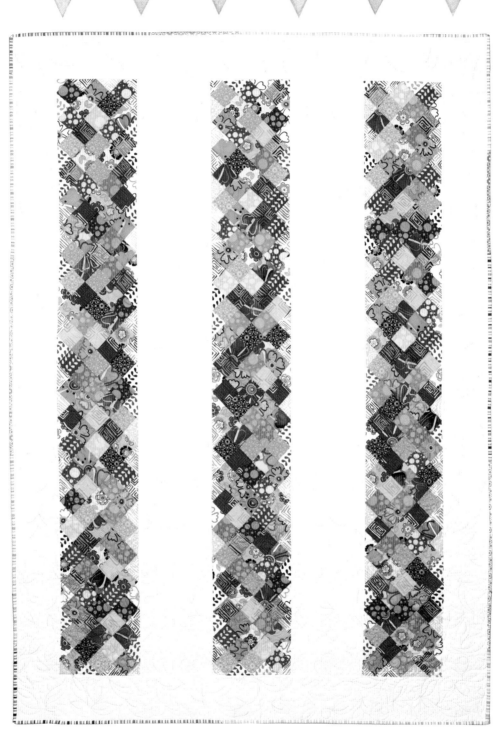

Carnival Confetti Quilt

Quilt designed and made by Jean Ann Wright
Jelly Roll fabrics: Ticklish by Me and My Sister Designs for Moda Fabrics

6. From 4 bright jelly roll strips, cut each strip into (5) 2-1/2" x 7-1/2" rectangles for a total of 20 rectangles. You will use 18 of these rectangles for end strip units.

7. From 2 light or white jelly roll strips, cut a total of (10) 2-1/2" x 7-1/2" rectangles.

8. Choose (3) 2-1/2" x 7-1/2" bright rectangles and (2) 2-1/2" x 7-1/2" light rectangles. Sew the rectangles together with a light rectangle on each outside edge as shown. Press to make an end unit strip set. Make 2 end unit strip sets. Carefully cut the strip sets into (6) 2-1/2" end units.

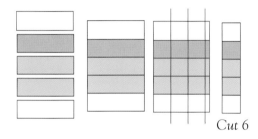
Cut 6

9. From a remaining bright jelly roll strip, cut (6) 2-1/2" squares. Cut any remaining portions of the light strips into 2-1/2" squares.

10. Sew light 2-1/2" squares to opposite sides of a bright 2-1/2" square. Sew an additional light 2-1/2" square to one side as shown to make a corner end unit. Make 6 corner end units.

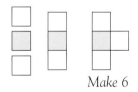
Make 6

Quilt Assembly

1. Separate the strip sets into three random color groups of (20) 2-1/2" x 10" strips.

2. Sew the strips sets together offsetting each row by one square as shown.

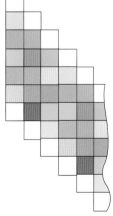

3. Referring to the Row Assembly Diagram, sew an end unit strip to opposite ends of each row. Sew a corner end unit to opposite ends of each row.

4. Using a rotary cutter and ruler, square up the sides and ends of each pieced row as shown. Take care to allow a 1/4" seam allowance on all sides.

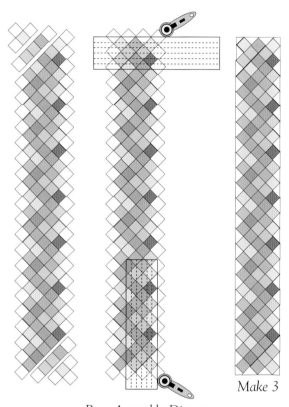
Make 3

Row Assembly Diagram

5. Measure a pieced row vertically from top to bottom. The measurement should be approximately 57"-58" long. From the white fabric, cut (2) 8-1/2" x length of the row measurement rows. Sew the 3 pieced rows and 2 white rows together to complete the quilt center.

6. From the white fabric, cut (2) 6-1/2" x length of the row determined in step 5 side borders. Sew the side borders to opposite sides of the quilt center.

7. Fold the quilt in half, top to bottom before measuring the width. Measure the quilt from side to side at the fold line to determine its width. The measurement should be approximately 55". From the white fabric, cut (2) 6-1/2" x width of the quilt top/bottom border strips. Sew these borders to the top and bottom of the quilt center to complete the quilt top.

Finishing

1. Layer the quilt top, batting and backing. Baste the layers together. Hand or machine quilt as desired.

2. Sew the remaining bright jelly roll strips together end-to-end to make one continuous binding strip. Fold the strip in half lengthwise with wrong sides together and press. Bind the quilt edges to finish.

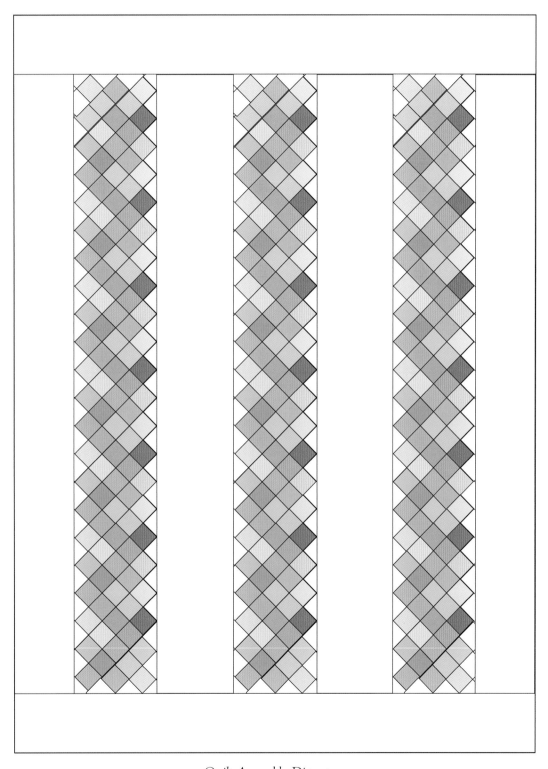

Quilt Assembly Diagram

Chicken & Seafood Jambalaya

Jambalaya is a great one-pot meal that can have a bit of everything in it. Meats can be a combination of anything that walks, crawls, flies, or swims. There are two basic varieties for a jambalaya recipe: Creole-style with tomatoes or Cajun-style without tomatoes.

This recipe includes ham, Andouille (sausage), chicken, shrimp and crabmeat. You can choose to have just seafood jambalaya with shrimp, crabmeat and oysters instead of the chicken. Seafood jambalaya will use a seafood stock instead of a chicken stock. For meat only jambalaya increase the amount of chicken and ham. This recipe calls for nearly 5 cups of a variety of meat and seafood. Adjust accordingly if you want to limit your jambalaya to meat and/or seafood only.

There are many jambalaya spice mixes if you prefer to use a prepared spice instead of making your own. Check your grocery store spice section and choose a favorite.

This recipe provides generous servings for 8. Jambalaya is delicious reheated and served as leftovers the next day.

Ingredients

2 tablespoons butter or olive oil

2 cups chopped onions

1 cup chopped celery

3/4 cup chopped green peppers

2 teaspoons minced fresh garlic

2 bay leaves

6 medium or 5 large fresh tomatoes, peeled and chopped

1 cup tomato sauce

2 cups uncooked rice

3 cups chicken broth

3/4 cup chopped ham

1/2 cup chopped Andouille sausage
  (use pork smoked sausage if Andouille is not available)

1/2 cup chopped chicken

1-1/2 cup chopped crabmeat

1-1/2 dozen peeled medium shrimp

2 bay leaves, crushed or ground

1/2 teaspoon dried thyme

Jambalaya Spice

1/4 teaspoon dried or ground sage

1 teaspoon file powder

1/4 teaspoon dry mustard powder

1/2 teaspoon freshly ground black pepper

1/2 teaspoon cracked pepper

1/2 teaspoon lemon pepper

1 teaspoon salt (optional)

Cooking

1. Heat the oil in a large, heavy pot (cast iron works best). Add the Andouille sausage, onions, green pepper, celery and garlic. Cook until vegetables are tender.

2. Add chicken broth, tomatoes, ham, and jambalaya spice. Simmer for 15 minutes.

3. Bring ingredients to a boil and add the rice. After adding the rice reduce to a simmer, cover and let it simmer for about 15 minutes.

4. Check to see if more broth is needed. If so, add the broth then cover and simmer for another 15 minutes.

5. Let the pot simmer until the rice is done. Turn off the heat and let the jambalaya sit in the pot for a few minutes to allow all the flavors to set in, but don't let it cool too much. Serve very warm.